Weekend Getaway at Generic Hotel

Brian Wood

SAKURA PUBLISHING

Alhambra, California

USA

Weekend Getaway at Generic Hotel

Brian Wood

Weekend Getaway at Generic Hotel

Copyright © 2017 by Brian Wood

skpublishing124@gmail.com

www.sakura-publishing.com

Special discounts are available on quantity purchases by corporations, associations, and others. For details, contact the publisher at the address above.

Book Interior Editing and Design by Derek Vasconi

First Edition

Printed in the United States of America

ISBN-10: 0-692-80053-0

ISBN-13: 978-0-692-80053-9

PRAISE FOR BRIAN WOOD'S FIRST BOOK, *WINTER WALK*

"Brian Wood is the kind of poet who reminds me of my favorites (Larkin, Frost, Auden). His poems have a meter, and form, and a classicism that is missing from most modern poetry. His words have a refreshing resonance that reaches far beyond what you see on the page. I enjoy them a great deal."

-Thomas Trofimuk, Author of *Waiting for Columbus*

"Any man who loves dogs and words, especially together, is someone I like. Anyone who uses those words as Brian Wood does in this collection of his poems, I admire. There are questions here, some with answers, all provoking. There are moments here we have all felt, both of helplessness and of surprising inner strength. Take a walk with his dogs and his words—you'll find it refreshing."

-Roy MacGregor, Author of *Northern Light*

"Brian Wood is the genuine article—a serious poet whose mastery of language and form stand out among his contemporaries. Beautiful lines, cadenced, measured, and often angular, characterize poems that invite re-reading, just to savor the turns of phrase."

David L. Jeffrey, FRSC

"I have been teaching English poetry since 1994 and I can tell you: this guy is the real thing. Blurbs are forever saying this kind of stuff, but really, he is seriously good. At his best, his work belongs in anthologies."

-Janice Fiamengo, University of Ottawa

ACKNOWLEDGEMENTS

Derek Vasconi, MH Clay, Johnny R Olson, David L Jeffrey, Katherine Jeffrey, Jordan Richerson, Gerald Lynch, Nicholas Von Maltzahn, Kim & Doug Stringer, David Rampton, Janice Fiamengo, David Solway, my brother, James Duthie, Bob McKenzie, Ken Reid, Michael Landsberg, Roy MacGregor, Danielle Payne, Noel Walker, my parents, Patty Mack, Hudson Mack, Colleen Jones, Katie Baker, Sean McIndoe, Sean Pronger, Ian Mendes, Mike Rehill, Catherine Hill, Christine Bird, Mark Leier, Nick Garrison, Amy Black, Nicole Winstanley, Thomas Trofimuk, William B Davis, Al Strachan, Michael Holmes, Joseph Planta, Kelly Bailey, Christopher Kevlahan.

DEDICATION

For Rachel, meridiana face di caritate.

Table of Contents

PROSE

YORBA LINDA

The tour guide, who knows his stuff cold, pauses for the laugh on the way. "Of course, Pat said it was Julie who named the dog." Some of the folks nod, not catching all of this, and not sure if it was in the movie. Waving us into the next room, we are shown the posters for the Senate campaign, which he won. "And Ike noticed him. In fact, Ike picked him for VP, and he was VP until 1961. Follow me here, please?" We stand loosely bunched. "To my right, you can see the 'Checkers' speech in a continual loop." We nod again, listening to our guide and the speech at the same time. "It was his first great crisis." More nodding. We are not told that this "crisis" soured our subject for the rest of his life, making him quite nasty. He was already paying a price for Alger Hiss; he'd pay it again. He'd never be absolved for being right.

And now The China Trip, as if shaking Chou's hand healed all the world. If you like this, there's more: a sort of Big Blowhard Hall Of Fame, some standing alone, some forever in a fake chat. Our subject had met them; each great leader is greater than the last. Our guide explains that all the statues are "exactly life-size." We see them up close: de Gaulle tall and hooked, Yoshida a turncoat's turncoat, Brezhnev somehow still dumber than he seemed, and Mao right up front, Moloch among evil. Chou is just to his side, drinking in the wisdom of that man in sin, who recked not.

In the next room, our guide knows what's coming and deflects it with skill. "People see me before the tour," he says, chuckling, "And say, in hushed tones, are we going to....you know, talk about you-know-what? And I say....of course we are!" He waits out the laugh, again timing it perfectly. "Watergate happened. So let's talk!" He gives a careful

1

summary of a break-in out of nowhere, who might have ordered what. In the background you can hear Ehrlichman tell the President they're going for a 'limited modified hang out.' We finish in the study, where he worked on books, rehabilitating his life, and, he hoped, name. Except the name will always mean covering up, as he said himself, a failed burglary. Then quitting, too late, in a speech tough to watch even now. Self-pity consumed him as fire through parched wood.

At the end, I clap along with the others, and ask our guide if he liked the latest hit film about our subject. "No, too many mistakes with the record. What was your take?" I shrug and say no one will ever root out this man's substance. He smiles the smile of a former cop, which he is. "Vic," he says, shaking my hand. Answering a question I don't ask, he volunteers that working here keeps him from trouble. His face says he knows something about trouble. Once he learns my name, he repeats it, as cops do. He tells me I shouldn't miss the Birthplace, where we hear a taped voice say "I was born in this house, built by my father, on January 9, 1913, in Yorba Linda. This land has much changed."

Nothing in the house is different from other boring museum homes. Nothing here tells you that a (sometimes) great and good man lived there, undone by hand, his own. He gave his enemies bright, gleaming swords, and he'd polished them himself. Each night he would sharpen by stone. When they did come, when they thrust it into his neck, did he smile, since he had forged the steel, and he knew the blade fast, and the aim true?

July 2015

Weekend Getaway at Generic Hotel

COUPLE ON A BENCH WITH TWO BORED DOGS

If you could find the path, you'd go looking for it and keep walking until you were too tired to go on. The trail is not marked, but once on it, you can see all the way from Eagle Island to the eastern edge of a half circle bay. The path was cut from a mountain and warnings of rockfall are posted on piles of stones. You would walk next to huge alders, cedars and spruce on guard against a tall spring sun. Hundreds of white sailboats make a big blue ocean seem bigger still. On a short break from our walk, we sit on a bench made from a log right by Nelson Creek and watch water rushing over stone. Something to see forever.

And since we don't have much to say just now, I wonder, is there anything better than the silence of two people in love? Is being any sweeter unsaid? If this were a new movie, there'd be light strings playing, as the breeze toyed with your hair. I'd say things funny and true and deep and you'd nod, knowing I meant it. The camera would catch your hand deftly slipping into mine. The dog splashing in the water would stumble and fall on to your lap, and we'd both laugh, and after that, all problems solved. True love at last. And in a bad movie you'd die of something vague in Act IV... and the event, so cruel, would change me. I'd learn what death only can teach: what we thought was perfect could endure, here, just briefly.

I'm glad we're not that film; and there is no way to tell you, in any words that could be numbered, how happy I am right now, in these trees by a pooling creek. I would not trade two minutes with you on this beat up old log for any clumsy fiction about love. And what we have could never be captured by some hack's dull formula, but only pictured by ideas not seen

3

yet, fanfares in the dreamy spheres. These lines only show a faint trace and perhaps you are not meant to be taken in whole, since your face is the sun at ease, strolling the sky in summer.

As when we met, and I saw nothing but high, bright noon, and the light stretching out wide across a stony plain.

May 2013

1st CHURCH OF COQUITLAM

The church with a sign just like a new bank's faces the mall and blends right in, God and Mammon making a compact after all. Two miles away, The Coquitlam Centre for Worship refuses to call itself a church, name whom they worship, or why. They offer round-the-clock daycare and not a sermon but a weekly "message" from a Reverend Steve, presumably the poor man's presbyter. And they are a stone's throw from The Port Moody Bible House, also, for sure, not a church. Their sign says the lattes and scones are the best in town. Thursdays, you can get two for the price of one.

And if some of this recalls your childhood, where giving was expected to be ten percent of the net, and tax receipts handed out each spring, maybe it's cause to wonder if what Jesus died for fell out of the sky, and the people lost their sight, and just the names survive now, a way of speaking, and that to vanish next. When the son of the morning goes for walks near my house, a mere stroll from yours, he must take great joy in the Not A Church at the bland mall, whose bright orange sign fits in so seamlessly, in the world and of it. But will his victory seem boring or quaint if, on the day he declares sovereign rule, half of the celebrants don't notice, and the rest don't care, so long as the coffee stays hot, each week poured by a friendly face?

October 2014

Brian Wood

BLOCK PARTY PLANNING MEETING

Hi, good morning! I'm Tod Kirk: I run the Sunday Life Groups
here, at Coquitlam House Of Something Or Other. It's nice to
meet you. Coffee is over there, plus snacks. A membership
pays for itself in a month; try the dark roast. Join me in class
today? My text is from Matthew, and I show my students that
'salt of the earth' was just a simile; back then, they didn't know
what we do. Next week, we're having a picnic instead of class,
and the week after that, it's movie night. We're showing the one
where the security guard gets trapped in the museum. Not in
the mood for class? No problem. Can you stay for our
gathering? Once we had services but brevity means we're out
by noon sharp; Jake likes to say we are a new priesthood of
believers.

There's a guest messenger today: Martin Cauvin. Those are his
blu-rays and books out here for sale, some of them at half
price. You can make it? Great, sit right beside me. The...what?
Hymnal? No, we don't need them here. We'll do some praise
songs first, and by "we," I mean the rock band up front. The
bassist went to Juilliard for a year and then heard his Call. Now
our lead worship manager—Jake—you will love this guy—
no—the one with the Leafs cap—reads out what's happening
this week. If gatherings aren't your style, our teens play floor
hockey on Tuesdays and have Tweetups on Fridays. Our Men's
Group plays golf on weekends and basketball in the gym on the
first. (It used to be Men's Fellowship but they ran out of time
for that.) Are you married? Ladies' Prayer Group reads a new
book in the winter and then talks it out over spring, summer
and fall. I think this month they're reading—or watching—
House of Sand and Fog. And on the tenth we plan our block
party.

Weekend Getaway at Generic Hotel

I'll be quiet now, for the offering, our band prefers total silence
while they do their Zeppelin covers. What will Martin Cauvin
say? Oh, he's great. Here he is now. See you in the lobby?
Please, sit. This is the kind of place I like, a real house of God.
Yet our young people today have so many distractions before
them: instant money, instant sex, instant fame: Warhol himself
would blush at what passes for fame in our day. How can we
expect our youth to stay true to God if we don't stay true to
them? And still we stick to our old words, our old scripture,
our old praise. I say this by command: we must be born anew,
we must diligently teach our children, true defenders of the
faith. How can we make safe the word of God if it's not the
same word as our neighbors? Who will come if they don't? I
thank the Lord always, rejoicing, that my children could not
tell my own church from the nearest pub or rec center. Far
enough away they are one. I...what? HEAR, O ISRAEL: THE
LORD OUR GOD IS ONE LORD....*Excuse me. Thanks for*
the invite to movie night. Each book of mine is half-price.

March 2015

Brian Wood

PLEASE DRINK RESPONSIBLY

The couple beside us at the breakfast place is half cut well
before noon. Their talk is just argument, loud and unflinching.
They aren't listening and don't care if you are. "Fuck, our food
is late. Shit, it's packed. Fuck, not my problem. Where's that
beer? Go call me a cab. What? Shit, not them. Fuck." They sip
from their drinks without pleasure and neither has smiled once,
even briefly, at anyone or anything. Her taxi shows up at
twelve and he, I guess, staggers out after he's finished the
beers.... The ads for liquor sell cool, success, money, sex right
now and forever. At no point do they show the half-stewed
couple swearing at each other over their menus, both of them
making you wish you left ten minutes ago.

Just what the f—k happened here? Were they in love once,
deeply, and then said things you can't take back? And today,
stuck in a hopeless choked zugzwang, a stalemate unto death.
When did they choose cheap beers over even a bleak parody of
love? You'd ask them, but their eyes are bottles, just waiting
for bigger drinks at home, where they need not sip. They must
take in enough to forget any nice gift, any grace note, or maybe
that day in Stanley Park they spoke hushed vows, English Bay
as blue witness, tall cedars nodding.

They strike at each other now, hissing, the booze taking away
what little there was. No late kindness to sweetly mix with that
memory of a rainy walk in the fall, when just holding hands
was enough. They're unknowing, unwilling stand-ins, showing
us how man was made for hell, its refuse forged in our image.
They fight to the death, all of us a hostage, getting to see up
close the wages of sin, the high, high heat, and what you would
give to break free.

January 2015

WHAT! ARE YOU HERE?

You come at the strangest of times, unasked, and I will be lazily surfing channels, bored at the store, stuck in traffic, on the phone with someone I barely know, and then years dissolve, and though your body is gone, your voice is suddenly clear and I hear it all day. You went without asking and that I can never forgive you for.

It is a deep secret I share with no one, how angry I am you left without my say so, that you thought it was somehow ok to become spirit only, and not ask me.

It was never ok. It still isn't and I burn white hot: there is nobody to tell you that grief is part hate, hating what happened, always hating it, and forgiving, forgetting, just not possible.

Still, your offstage voice feels like rushing snowmelt on the hottest, closest August day. I am in hell but these brief visits of yours make it seem like the gates could be swung clear. When you say to me, 'The hurt will stay but might sting less,' I nod yes, having no choice, knowing what I want, you here forever, was taken away three years ago. And if today is a mere show, my mind's trick to hide what I can't help, then I accept, since just saying your name is spring water sprinkled on a parched soul, who wandered in Saharas far too long.

June 2013

Brian Wood

SULLIVAN CABERNET RESERVA PRIVEE DE KAMLOOPS

Welcome to Sullivan Estates, my private winery here in
Kamloops, or K-town, as I call it. See that lawnmower over
there? A gift from one of the guys on "The Beachcombers." I
do some of my best radio programming up here, up in the barn,
away from the big city and generic wine. I call my show
"Sullivan's Hodgepodge," just a few songs each week. I get
letters every year from listeners, some from as far away as E-
Town. Edmonton. You'd be surprised at how many people start
their day with the "Hodgepodge." Man, the Mamas And Papas
knew the score; why don't today's kids "get" it? Or take Peter,
Paul and Mary: better than all that loud rap and metal. They
were for peace. Who isn't? One time I interviewed Joni
Mitchell for the *Saanich Irregular* but she claims she doesn't
recall. They have no time for you once they are famous. I
waved to her, once, at the Beverly Hills, but she thought I must
be Ben Mulroney. I've covered all their shows, and I met them
all on the way up. Bryan, Joni, Alanis, Justin, Nelly, Sarah,
Michael. Buble can sing, man, but he calls me by the wrong
name all the time. It's our private joke and I'm not sure why he
isn't laughing. Kids today—need more wine? This is Sullivan
Private Reserve Cabernet—mostly know me from movies, not
TV. So long ago. I was a detective in the one where Jodie won
the Oscar. On junkets she calls me, to this day, Gerry, which is
close enough. Tough for people to remember when you have
three names. Gerry is just fine, really.

On the Fox show where Johnny Depp got his start, I was the
dead guy in season one and the vain drama teacher in season
two. I was starting to show my range. For some reason every
CD wanted me to play the bad cop, but I said "No, man, that's
not my scene." What? CDs are casting directors. I got to know

10

a lot of them, back when I still auditioned. Now *they* call me. Just last week I played a self-absorbed drama teacher in a new show called "Pretty Girls At Fake College."

Have you seen it? It's on every other Friday at 7. No. In the morning. Anyway, you're here to ask about my book, "Hodgepodge: The Book." Let me top that up for you. Try the cheese, a personal gift from the hotel in Santa Monica that lost my reservation during the daytime Emmys. My book? Right. Dude, back in the day, radio meant something. We'd play our tunes, we didn't care what the Man said. Rock ruled. That's a photo of me getting high three feet away from Jefferson Airplane on their one gig in Squamish. Once they sobered up, and got paid in full, they played a free half-hour show for Greenpeace. That's what the kids don't get now. Values. Funny, the guys in "Airplane" called me Barry too, which, again, is *fine*. Close enough.

When you are Perry Saul Sullivan, after awhile you live with the fact that your fame endures, and people are full of envy, whether it's the lawnmower from Jack, the private wines from Aykroyd, or the poster Sarah signed for me in '86. People just know that I'm set apart, a brighter flame, even if I have to tell them that "The Beachcombers" was on for almost twenty years.

March 2015

Brian Wood

SMARTIES BLIZZARD

If Sundays now are football and glad I am not in church, then yesterday I was, each week, and you'd find me there rain, snow or shine. The fairest of fair days at summer's peak, and still we'd be inside a windowless building, praising his Majesty. As my father did, I played in our small church band, he because he wanted to, me because it beat sitting and staring. He was our lead trombone, a bright, tuneful player (he sang that way too, taking the tenor on all hymns and "O Canada" at the rink). My own trumpet was clear but wild, that all knowing teen who needed no proof of his own gifts. We opened with "How Great Thou Art," then were silent and listened. Youth group now at eight. Potluck Tuesdays moved to Thursdays. Dorcas members, see Carol after church. Next week, elections for the church board, and…yes…remember, park only in the back of the lot, not in the marked spots up front.

Our director, who'd copied out all our parts by hand, cued us by rifling through a book called "Praise Hymns," and we'd be set for 'Stand with me, please.' She would nod at us, stage-whisper "Watch the key change to B flat!" and only the idiot trumpeter would miss it. To my left our bassist got it right each time. Behind me, Tim played a cornet meant to go unremarked. It worked. Phil had the drums and got it wrong every time. Our set list was before pop and its tempi and he never solved it. The answer was playing softly, and sometimes he abstained altogether. To my right was our lead clarinet, who when she sang was a week of freezing rain in June, but could make any small reed do her bidding. What were forests of sharps and flats to me were clear rhapsodies to her, river water leaping over rock.

Weekend Getaway at Generic Hotel

While ushers passed around felt-bottomed plates, we'd often play "Spirit of God, Descend Upon My Heart" (a tune that knows something of grief). Dismissed, we'd file out by choir chairs near the back. Everyone but me found a pew somewhere; I'd leave and walk half a mile for Smarties mixed with 'vanilla soft serve,' and stroll back through the foyer, my Pyrrhic revolt. People did and did not see this, depending on how amused they were.

How do you train a child in the way he should go, when he would be anywhere else? Some catch faith as kingfishers catch fire and others just do not care. In any event my own doubts were doubly useless: most churches are coffee shops now, God very much non compris. Their signs say "Grow, Connect, Serve," or FREE RE-FILLS, and if none of this reminds us of a man nailed to wood, legs broken, screaming "Eli, Eli," then it could be what I rebelled against gave up, and the light of the world went out.

December 2015

Brian Wood

A THOUSAND TONGUES SING

Some field you don't know in Cesena, Italy. A thousand people
you don't know waiting for the maestro to say "Andiamo." He
does and they do. Your ears twitch up, your soul somersaults,
over and over. The blood tingles and you tap along with foot or
hand. You'll stop smiling about this sometime next week. Four
hundred people sing the words to "Learn To Fly," by the Foo
Fighters. Two hundred bassists play the bass line just as
recorded, no mean feat.

It is a happy wall of sound on sound. Two hundred guitarists
pound out the riffs. Most magic of all, two hundred drummers
play the same beats for the whole four minutes, no one goes
out of tune or tempo, tough enough with a band of four, let
alone one thousand. Even tougher to say why the soul leaps up
at this and wishes you were there to play or sing along; why
this concert draws you in.

In a garden once a serpent fooled us, and we were never the
same, and our human trail, our ability to make any place hell, is
all over where you live and where I live. No thing or feeling a
human can't ruin, no place a human can't foul. But then the
soprano sings "Che soave zeffiretto," and for a few minutes the
shackles fall off and we see the world with new clear eyes, the
ones we had until just the other day; or an actor, his eyes hot,
says "Angels are bright still, though the brightest fell," and our
spine feels the chill for years, treasuring each syllable; or these
folks gather in a field, and if only briefly, make this world
shake, our goodness unbound, infinite, not here anymore,
hearts free, souls at play.

August 2015

14

THE RED DETACHMENT OF WOMEN

Kill me now. I am chief "art critic" of the Beijing Free Press, tasked to cover this bilge, except I won't call it that and nor will my colleagues. Not the ones who like to breathe. Mao's latest whore wrote it, so we'll wax rhapsodic over each word, note, and plot point. Because my mother once hinted to her college class that there was a chance the Great Helmsman might not be correct at all times, now and forever, she was "reformed" in a local prison, dead a few days later. They honored my father deeply, with a special dunce cap, parading him around town like a moron. He received still more honor, a Red Guard "critical" session, and no one knows where they chucked the body. I myself was sent out to the countryside, to be purged of Mozart, Keats, and Dante, artists who were, at best, sure not the Chairman. Once I was pronounced pure enough to beg for my life, I was sent back to the city, to this paper, where I say Mao's words moved a nation, and I limn his latest whore's praises. She knew of my mother, vaguely; that's why my parents were so severely "educated." It's why she picked me to write the program for tonight; my job is to distill her gifts so that mere citizens can still get the gist.

And here it is. Plot Point Number One: Bad Foreigners invade China. You can spot them with ease: they scowl, wear dirty clothes, smoke, and sell dope. They push drugs on a pure populace. Plot Point Number Two: the Bad Foreigners, constantly citing Adam Smith or Burke, are driven out of China by Detachment Twenty of the Red Guards, an army of women, that is, women inspired by absolute truth, that is, Mao's new...that is to say, Jiang Qing *nu shi*. We know they are Good because each one has a little red book and speaks its clichés.

15

That's the plot. I'll let you imagine the music and words. The big hits in this show, the songs that get the most forced applause, are "Be aware of rightists," "Fight liberalism," and "To study a problem is to solve it."

Anyway, don't worry about me. My review will glow, and the harlot will take note. It's the others I worry about. Peng is being educated tonight, again, and we'll hear the screams. Lin will be criticised for a week, and then his plane will have a problem, and just maybe they find the corpse. Even Chou will die in a spare ward out of the way, our Chairman not lifting a finger. This the happy fate of old *tongzhi* from the Long March. Picture what he does to enemies.

When a man becomes God, truth runs and hides and never really comes back. Come to my country and see: his large flat face on murals, in the great public squares, even, in a nice touch, on our money…. Someday they will string the old whore high, high up in the air, and a rope will swing, and a knife will sever; and that will be good. But who can resurrect all those she purged? And those purified by her husband—can the numberless be made whole? Even a Daniel come to judgement is rendered mute here, forever speechless.

June 2015

WHAT IT'S LIKE BEING PRESIDENT

It is strange, this work of being a man and a nation. When I took the oath six years back, I became not just me but this country. I was its face. I would fly to other lands and my mere presence stood for USA. Until there was a new president, for better or for worse, I was us. This is one thing abroad and another here. Away, people in foreign countries hold back a bit, give you the benefit of not knowing for sure. At home there are no doubts. Millions did not vote for me and never would, and the millions who did mean nothing. We love our country so much we forget others might. Voting for not-my-guy is the wrong vote, not just thinking different. Something like that in every soul. Millions hate me and more millions yet will hate my successor. To get this job is to accept free-flow hate, hate looking for home, boiling over, hissing. I could give a speech saying water was wet and my mail next day will be full of stuff about how my kids can rot in hell, my wife can go there too, plus you hope my dog gets killed. So I (kind of) look forward to the head of state days, when I am more symbol than man.

Today though is its own challenge, at the Veterans' hospital, giving what aid I can to our soldiers injured on my watch. Some will live and some will sleep. I talk with those who would and read to men whose speech has stopped. A little boy asks me why I weep, but no words come. Together we read his father's citation for bravery. We say it again and then a third.

On my way out, a Marine's mother holds her hands up, defiant—"Why does YOUR child live, while mine rots in Arlington?" I start to speak but wisdom tells me to be still. Her words are white hot and far from done and far from quiet. She calls me every foul word she knows and this is when all of my staff stops hoping to be president. The man in me revolts at this

Brian Wood

but the nation that lives in me must stand and wait. I stare into a fury undiminished. My role is to take this, be the face of wrong, and everything wrong with everything, our first sin and last bad act, living proof nothing here could ever break right. Now her husband can only take so much grief, and leads his wife into the closest chair; his eyes have some pity, man to man, but on my watch, on my watch, he lost his son, and I must know the wages.

On our way home my staff says little. I say less, except "That woman hates me with an undying fire." No one disagrees. I wonder if tonight, when I see her son in sleep, when I see him wandering in the shades, if my sight will be pierced by the salvation we hope saves all those who fell by faith, or my eyes blinded by the freedom purchased at so high a price by soldiers sent too far away, and just one day too long.

April-May 2015

WEDDING DAY

Twenty chairs, facing west. A small table up front and the local registry on top of that. The seats slowly fill and the groom and I guess a minister take their places (or they will... soon). People smile pleasantly. Evidently nobody rehearsed.

On some kind of unseen cue, the bride's sister presses 'play' and soon Handel's very soft seventh keyboard suite can be heard, making its case for beauty, order and a perfect world. You could listen to this forever, or you could watch as the bride makes her way in, stepping carefully. Her smile a reminder love has no ending, and without it, there is no life. For whatever reason, she said yes.

And here we are, on this late July Saturday by the ocean, with twenty friends and our kind of minister. He reads, none too surely, the short vows we asked him to say. To break this up, a gifted actor we know recites short verses from Auden and Rossetti, and our small group sits back, pleased. But it is hearing "I do, I will" that gets the biggest response, and for reasons unknown to me the exchanging of rings makes everyone start. You soon become all eye, trying to capture everything in your mind forever, clearer than pictures.

There must be something in a wedding clearer than life itself, for today even the shy smile like a rhapsody, and everything everyone says is funny, and the music is slowly swept by breezes in drowsy harmony, and sunlight keeps bubbling up, up, up.

Rachel, today the winds off the ocean trail thru your hair and curl away into forever. As if we two, whispering up front our simple vows, have stumbled into striking bright possibility.

December 2013

Brian Wood

WHEN RED LILIES LAST IN THE DOORYARD BLOOM'D

It may be that certain days or times carry the real weight of
love, like some days feel colder or hotter than others, damn the
thermometer. And the calendar acts as a buffer, keeping us
from thoughts too heavy for all year. So they still give us a
glancing blow, they still sting, on some days, memories we
swore we'd tamed. Love can never be out of motion or shaped,
but we like to forget that, and tell ourselves we can move on,
mature.

And then a day comes and we can't breathe. No blue sky can
shift it. Years become moments, and just now we are at the
hospital, saying goodbye, the nurse looking away. How can
something so deep in the past be yet raw, delicate to the touch?
How can a feeling, so lost, outlast monuments?

Rachel, "ever returning spring, trinity sure to me you bring,"
and you can never know what I'd give to wipe out what
happened fifteen years ago. I'd blot it, remove it, have it
expunged, or alter it, the way they used to in the old communist
photos, where Comrade A suddenly ceased to be.

In my new picture, death and your father would be in room 342
of the hospital, talking. And Death would know. Death would
depart. He would lay down a new law. They would talk long
into the spring night, one of them opening the window, sharing
a glass or two of whisky. Death would nod, appreciating the
brand and just the right amount of ice. And they'd keep talking,
and seeing your father's tall white flame grow hotter, stronger,
Death would raise his last glass once, and our new clear eye
could see your father's shade slip out that window, whole and
entire, his burning flame free, and free now, today. And in
some night I can't dream and you can't prophesy, he will come

Weekend Getaway at Generic Hotel

in a vision, and it will just be the two of you on a long drive somewhere, laughing, both of you unable to stop. No need to.

And he will tell you the last enemy he destroyed was death.

And you say yes, knowing he was right.

April 2015

Brian Wood

IN THE WAITING ROOM

I am at the hospital, have been for some time. My wife is three rooms down, dying. That's been going on awhile too. Last week when I held her hand she grasped it, but now I'm not sure she knows I'm here. I could handle this, or some of it, if it wasn't for our friends. They have come in droves and most of them I would wish away in a blink.

"I guess God needed another angel, eh?"

"She'll be with Jesus soon."

"The parking here is awful."

"Don't dwell on it."

"I know just how you feel."

"God never gives you a problem you can't handle."

Do these people not *hear* themselves? At least in a few hours she will be spared the sound of chatter for its own sake. When will we learn to be still? God did give me a problem: I don't know whether to forgive these folks or give them the beating they so richly deserve. But it would help nothing.

On my way in, to fix my wife's pillow and hold her hand one last time, and tell her she was whatever it is that makes a sky blue, and streams of water rush cold and clear, John, a friend from school, takes me aside, wanting to know where he can validate…Lord, save him, and teach him the gift of silence. Since today, three rooms from here, present is transformed into past. For her sake, forgive what he presumably cannot help. At six, they close the curtains in all the rooms. Her race ran its full course; let her enter your courts with praise.

August 2013

OUR CHURCH HAS ONE FOUNDATION

We are the hands and feet of Christ. We meet each Sunday at ten and Tuesdays at seven without fail. I sit towards the back and you sit near the front. My soul mixes with yours, and you are the motion of mine. We have been at this church forever and always will. We take up the sword of the Spirit against Satan and his works: in this small town, we are light deep in the forest.

Our fathers laid the cornerstone in 1900 and we've been coming ever since: Depression, war, trials of despair: we kept coming. What were our small disputes if our God reigned? Little mistakes meant nothing, because to do God's will means working through where good faith might err: The Lord was ours before we were the Lord's.

Until we broke up, that is, half of us turning away, since many of us had captured a taste for pure truth, the really correct doctrine, God's true plan; and the taste developed greatly. Soon I could see you weren't fit to teach our classes, and in a dream, you saw I couldn't be in the choir. You ceased to be my keeper, and I knew you could look out for yourself. If all this made a few cry, well, time they knew that some folks can't change for the better. Maybe I mean to say won't.

Anytime you want to apologize, look me up and I will listen, but chaff cut from the wheat has a way of staying chaff. Oh….I guess I miss you on Sundays, but on that day we chose whom to serve; God must have smiled on us, or you would not have rebelled, and there'd be no need to cast you out.

August 2015

Brian Wood

HEAVEN'S GATES AND HELL'S FLAMES

My friend and I amble up the aisle of a darkened church. A
spotlight has been trained on us as we move to the front. He
plays Construction Guy One; I play his sidekick, Construction
Guy Two. We go into our rehearsed patter. As per the script,
now I announce that I, for one, don't believe in God.
Construction Guy One stifles a laugh, drops his lunchbox,
takes off his hard hat, and sits me down for a chat about my
soul. The Lord can make me whiter than the snow frosting the
church windows. Since Construction Guy One always knows
better than I do, I accept, and we pray for salvation.

We get up to go on our way, but the audience can hear traffic
sounds, and my friend and I don't notice, and bam! It's all done
and we fall to the floor. A slight pause, the whole church now
dark, but when we do stand up, it turns out we made the right
call; and an austere angel, to the strains of the famous chorus,
points us to the right way. We yell and shout into eternity.

A lot of our friends aren't as lucky. In their sketches, they don't
accept the Lord, so when their traffic noises come, and they
don't get away in time either, they meet a quite different fate.
Now the grim angel points left, and off they go, kinda-
shrieking and sort-of-screaming, into the fake hell set. In case
we missed the message, when the make-believe is over, the
director booms through the speakers to say that tonight, any
night, could be it. We could perish this very evening, on the
way home from church; the Lord is here, in this room right
now. Salvation lay within. It was ours to grasp or refuse; the
choice, he said, pausing two or three beats, was clear.

And it was clear to him I think but not to me. The play stank.
No Marxist melodrama could have been more dull. Who makes
kids put on this bilge? The director and writer did not care for

24

Weekend Getaway at Generic Hotel

any of us in the youth group: we were just another bunch of idiots to teach parts to. Next week they'd have to do the same lines with a gaggle of not-all-that-helpful teenagers. And the whole year; it's how they made their living. How they could sleep at night, while taking money for what they thought of as God's work, I don't know.

When a belief becomes doctrine, can it be saved? In the early New Testament, we read of a love so strong it would rule the earth forever: but if you skipped ahead a few chapters, you'd see the book of Life, closed for good; and now a wrathful God, his mercy done, setting down an eternal judgement. That small church I went to made its voice clear—choose you this day whom you will serve.

And how sad it had to be that way, when just that morning, we heard, from someone we knew, of a law that said love could hold no memory. That if someone wronged you, you forgave him 500 times, and each time after that. Because to judge would make us no different...we'd build our house on the substance of a thing hoped for, and that if we could forgive as Christ did, our own sins would be cast into the depths of the sea.

October 2013

Brian Wood

MY LAST FAREWELL

Ray, this has got to sound spontaneous. Make sure Al knows that and he runs it by Bob. John, too. Don't send one to Mitchell; his wife is hopeless.... I hope I haven't let you down...

My fellow Americans, this is the last time I will address you from this place: the 37th time I have spoken to you from The Oval Office; I am your 37th President; these are the kinds of symmetrical things I was forever saying. *Try to smile and pause.* Friday, at noon eastern, Gerald Ford will be sworn in as President, in this office. To leave now is abhorrent to every instinct in my body.

How did it get to this? I did ok in this job: and until Watergate I was doing fine. Our war in Vietnam is done, *without the right-wingers here (and yes I mean you, Buckley) losing their minds.* I made peace with a quarter of the world. China is still an enemy but we must talk; you don't make peace with a friend. As for Israel and the nations who surround her, I laid down a structure of peace; it will not be perfect but someday the shooting must end. *Perhaps Anwar can let the healing start.*

I made a kind of permanent truce with Stalin's half-mad successors, men who lived through his terror and could see the police at night, coming.

Here at home I was a liberal's dream, which I won't address tonight. I will let others note that I passed bills to clean air and water; I gave Blue Lake back to the Taos Pueblo. I even proposed a guaranteed income for all Americans. But I talked the fool, played the fool, complained about welfare bums; I said all the wrong things after Kent State, all to keep Buckley's

26

gang happy. It worked: I crushed McGovern and I'd have crushed Gene, Shriver or Humphrey.

To those that supported me, even when it became unpopular to do so, I won't forget you. And to those that stood against me, I feel no bitterness. You did what I did to Hiss: in this game that counts as fair play. So I leave….I leave, let me make this clear, with no bitterness.

Colson, Colson. I could never stop my shouting and he would never stop smiling or nodding. The fool. Couldn't he see I was venting!!!??? No plan was too stupid or grandiose for Chuck, he approved it all. Tomorrow I become "ex-President" because he hired the world's dumbest burglars, idiots who couldn't use tape or figure out how telephones work. Trust CIA guys to get even the little things wrong.

If you will learn from me, learn this: hate is a raging fire which cannot be quenched; it destroys he who lights the fire and he who is consumed, and offence comes most when no offence is meant. You don't lose when you lose; you lose when you hate. So…I leave, as I say, with no bitterness…no need for your pity. The people who need our pity are the bored rich, the ones who have nothing but money, and nothing to do but spend and complain. That is the hottest circle.

I was a vile, short-tempered man who did great things for this country and the world. But you often find the greatest faults within the skin of the greatest men. And if I failed at least I failed while daring greatly. I wish you good night: and may God greatly bless the United States. *How did I do? Rose, this is too long, have Ray cut out the dull parts. Underline 'hottest' and 'daring.'*

May 2014

27

Brian Wood

LOVE SONG LATE IN THE 2ND YEAR OF MARRIAGE

(This is the second of our reign).

What flew through the air today was sight not sound, although the trees swayed anyhow, stunned. Light broke through these dull clouds late, as if even the air around us had had enough of brooding, scowling skies, skies with no light or hope. And my wife out there for a walk as a metaphor for all this, unplanned and unasked. For my long week she will find an excuse to treat me like I could be the only thing that matters, this instant and forever. On the most mundane Monday she finds ways to bring small lights and grace notes to a life otherwise contingent— deals on the phone with those not in my control.

Not all compacts endure. But this one does, its essence an ionic bond, and I can't wait till you come back, though it has been mere minutes. "My soul pants after you," as the psalmist said. There could be no other analogy, no other synecdoche, nothing on this earth has Rachel stand in for anything else.

Even metaphor gets only so close. No torch can teach you to burn bright. If there is the perfect word canvas, look at a prayer wheel, set on fire with hope, where others see only dark; picture a murmuration of starlings where others see only shapes against a late winter sky.

February 2015

2060 OGILVIE

You are flipping through a bunch of them, quite bored, not caring. You would give anything to be sleeping, but that will not come for hours, so you keep looking at these boring Facebook pictures of people you haven't seen in years, and, barring coincidence, won't ever again. At 2060 Ogilvie Road I would see them every day, and some of them on Sundays; they would see me too and no one was rejoicing.

Some sat behind me in History, some in front of me in French, others just to the left in Man In Society, and a few more sat where it pleased them during Music Appreciation. Under skilled torture by pros I could not tell you why I am looking at dull shots of people, all strangers now, back at my old high school, sipping ginger ale in The Eighties Room.

But I don't really wonder why they showed up, or why others will, next time. To sit in French 201 for ten months is to make a friend, willing or no; by June you know that person like the streets by your house. If nothing else, you finally figure out what Frost meant about good fences. Time plays her sly tricks, and we find out too late that the other inmates weren't so bad after all; they were just close. They didn't set the rules or have you serve your sentence.

And most of them were in your corner, some of them even cheering, as you found your way out of the place, knowing there'd be no worse time. They'd never be the one to tell the warden. And if they didn't cheer and didn't care, well, they, like you, had no choice. Their eyes were fixed on when that small hand would strike three pm, and the lucky ones didn't come back, even if in your dreams unlooked for, there you all are again, young, with no one of any idea what may come.

May 2014

Brian Wood

POEMS

Brian Wood

RACHEL SUITES

Allemande
The healing table laid just so. Jug of
Ice water, cooling pleasantly. Two
Different painkillers, both within easy
Reach. TV remote controls, all three
Of them, just to the right.

Courante
If you missed any of that, there's more:
A Nixon book one foot away, easily grasped—
And something else on the Long March
Nearby, on the closest shelf. You can
Tell Rachel was raised by a nurse,
But if you can't, beneath my healing
Table is a discreet unmarked brown
Puke bucket.

Sarabande
Love shoots out and manifests itself in
The world as it would. Checking it is like
Checking Niagara Falls; you can do it
But your success would be short-lived

33

Brian Wood

And fruitless.

Menuet I

The anaesthesiologist who met Rachel knew
She was up against a force. "I can tell...."
She said, trailing off. In my mind I finish
Her thought: "I can tell this woman is,
Despite herself, deeply in love. Nothing
Bad can happen to you while she is here
Or thinking of you. Nothing on earth escapes
This. She will protect you from all fates.
In heaven her light will make stars scarlet
With jealousy. In hell she will draw the shades,
Run the coldest shower, and stand there until your soul
Can rest."

Menuet II

Funny how she could tell all that from your
Eyes, which were bluer than usual and red-shot,
Doing your best to look bored. You could tell
I wanted out, now, and tried to act like I could
Handle it. I couldn't. I wanted to leave.

Weekend Getaway at Generic Hotel

Gigue

How can you fall in love, in summer on the
Prairies, again in Vancouver in fall, all
Over again in Montreal, in a museum
In California, and keep falling, deeper?
Why is holding hands in the hospital
Ratification of what can't be written down?
Rachel, to say I am a lucky man is to
Admit language is a beggar.
To say I love you is like saying the Pacific
Ocean waters the world and is an infinite blue.

November 2014

Brian Wood

FAITH HEALING 2015

All the old tricks in place, no real change. Still
The earnest toupeed man with the deep voice
Implores you to send him your money right
Now, in God's holy name. By faith alone
Can your small gift be made into the Lord's
Temple. Depressed? Sick? Simply call this toll
Free line and God, or his word on this earth,
Will answer. He shall supply all your needs.

Easy enough to laugh at these moron
Frauds and their idiot donors, each one
Dumber than the last. So who is calling
These numbers? Who builds these tributes to greed?
The poet said "In everyone there sleeps
A sense of life lived according to love:"
Nothing would ever shake it and nothing
Would cure it. For some lucky ones it all

Fits somehow and, being blessed, bless. Some flail
About for no cause, not caring whence they came
Nor where they go. And others— born into
A world far too severe—must watch The Man

Weekend Getaway at Generic Hotel

From Toupee in the hope he can bring what
They never found by things seen, and unseen
Things too far to help; as if part of man
Is programmed to be unhappy, and takes

No consolation from love past or love
To come, what they hold dear, or how bright their
Light might glow. As if part of us indites
The dark. Which could be how the preacher from
The Church Of The Airport Marriott sleeps
At night, knowing he fools no one who sees,
That his funds come from those so lost they trust
Cash sent by mail means a revelation,
One that was always good and always true.

September 2015

Brian Wood

CHRIS BURDEN (1946-2015)

What there was of me was you. The sense I
Mean, it took modernity to take my
Stuff and call it art. In Rembrandt's day they
Would have turned away or laughed, but now just
The best museums are fit for my craft.
Duchamp and others made me seem chic, and
Trust me, I had quite a bit of chic. I
Strung up a Porsche with a rock and called
It "Porsche With Meteorite." Then someone
Shot me in the arm and the title was
"Shoot." In my teaching days I'd tell my class
That art was what you thought of. I kept on.

You may have read about me in the back
Of the Times. Even the high toned priests there
Struggled with my work. They kind of asked—'What?!
Is this a joke? UCLA lets him
Be a professor?' But my cool made me
Untouchable, and all the right reviews
Announced I was a new kind of art, one
"That explored masculinity, martyrs
And the romantic notion of suffering

Weekend Getaway at Generic Hotel

For one's skill"….. And never mind nobody
Sane would give two cents for anything I
Said, did, or performed. In Chicago once

People paid to watch me not eat or drink
And I made it two days. That piece was called
"Doomed." A collection of toy soldiers I
Installed in mock war formation went by
"Tale of Two Cities." The Times? "Now Burden
"Explores postmodern anxiety." As
I say, no one wanted to spoil the fun.
I was famous where it mattered and art
Students knew my name. If the public did
Not, didn't that condemn them, not me? *Ars
Longa*, a teacher of mine used to say,
Which means art is the shape of my choosing.

Time will out. Listen: I have been dead not
Long and I am yet unused to this state.
What the sick see as great high walls the dead
See only as lines. Listen: I'm not sure
What to make of the one thing I did the
Public does like. People have got married
There, engaged too. In midtown LA I

Brian Wood

Cast "Urban Light," a forest of streetlamps
I restored for years. I painted them all
Grey and have them in the middle of a
Broad courtyard, not quite in straight rows. At dusk
They're all lit, and each night at six or so,

Especially on the weekends, hundreds
Come by to see what I wrought. I am stunned
By the words. "Oh! Beautiful! Some thing like
Paradise. Somehow so perfect." For once
My art spoken in praise, not irony;
And before I begin the night motions
Of all those no longer here, I catch one
More wedding about to start, right by the
Tallest lamp. Bride, groom, parents, two sets of
Friends, and of course their photographer, who
Is snapping, snapping, posing. Their delight
Seems evergreen. As joy would spring always.

Who was the muse here? Who set the flame? How
Can a lump of crap like me, who made his
Name peeing in buckets, get it just right?
My old prof had a line for that too—he'd
Say "Burden, even you have talent....You

Weekend Getaway at Generic Hotel

Never know." It could be I am proof that
Art picks it own voice, and cares nothing if
The artist is smart, dumb, kind, or selfish,
So long as he will not quit. He might be
Too slow to ever grasp his real gifts, yet
Just wise enough to get out of the way,
And light up forever the miracle mile.

May 2015

Brian Wood

CLASS STRUGGLE

When I was a child, I spoke as a child,
I understood as a child and would act
Out my own version of *Pilgrim's Progress*
On the beach, on vacation. My brother
Would get bored and wander off, so I'd be
Christian up against a Worldly Wiseman,
Fighting Giant Despair, and I'd walk the
Wall of Salvation. You know your childhood
Was odd when Bunyan is fun, yet he was
To me. At least I wasn't in school: the

Beach was better than another church, and
No more preaching for an instant, sweeter
Still. Blessed in many ways, I never feared
Mother would sneak drinks, or Father leaving
As soon as he could. I only feared what
I heard on Sundays, God's disgust with my
Sins; how all sin was the same sin, and you
Were as bad, if not worse, than your neighbor:
The Lord saw clean thru you; his hatred of
Sin was perfect, enduring forever.

Weekend Getaway at Generic Hotel

My wife, late one night, described playing "Class
Struggle" with her Dad. The board game had been
Invented by someone, I am guessing,
With way too much spare time and students who
Slept thru his *pensées*. Instead of what her
Friends played—where you moved pieces around a
Board and with any luck won all the deeds
To the hotels and the money and the
Railroads—Rachel did not get to pick a
Token, since "No one chooses which class they

Are born into." This game was severe: you
Lost points for pitying workers or blaming
Blacks or Jews. To win really big you had
To know your Marx, even the early pamphlets.
When she was a bad token all she could
Do was start wars or crush a union: the
Rules were strict. A good token meant she could
Be a shop steward who made ATU
Proud, whiter than snow, and got more rolls of
The dice for caring about poverty.

I wonder if her father actually
Enjoyed this game: Worker vs. Parasite

Brian Wood

Is always rigged one way or the other,
And, just like my Sunday school lessons, dull.
At some point in each life the child must wake
Up and know his mother human, and his
Father, fallible, and yet we seldom
See someone who truly breaks from what
They learned from the first teachers. My Father-
In-law had troubles with the unions.

They were rough with him, then rougher. But he
Made sure his daughter knew the words to Pete
Seeger songs and she'd never take work, or
The people who did real work, for granted.
I go to no church: and won't, and yet each
Poem of mine owes something to Psalms I
No longer sing. There's more to that book than
We see—the poet lays down his bed in
Hell, and "thou *art there*." No one outruns what
Made them new. Just today I get an email

From a studiedly neutral, carefully
Bi-partisan group, telling me there is
Still time to "Fight for a world that is fair
And just," a gospel learned from prophets, a

Weekend Getaway at Generic Hotel

Pure blazon that man must always mean more
Than money. And how good to see these words,
And fair and just are what we would most love,
Even if some of those prophets saw all
Too clear, and there'd be another great fall,
Leaving not one stone on a stone.

December 2014—January 2015

Brian Wood

WONDER WORKING POWER

On any Sunday morning in your mind,
Probably in winter, a man steps in
To a large baptismal font, or as we
Much preferred, tank. "The old now cast away
For the new. The old ways of sin now purged
For the new life of grace. Baptism just
An outward sign, but a sign nonetheless.
Let us pray." The rolled up shirt sleeves, in lieu
Of his normal jacket and tie, tell us
That today a few of us will put on

The incorruptible. "Jason, join me,
Would you?" Jason we have known for years and
Works part-time at the local Petro Can.
Nervous at first, he tells us why he's here.
"When my mother drank too much, we hid. My
Dad left early. He could not take it, so
My sisters and I, we kept hiding. Jill
Got married and so did Laurie. It was
Just me now, hard to hide when there's only
You. I came to this church because...." He points

Weekend Getaway at Generic Hotel

But doesn't need to. "I….Greg invited
Me." He motions his head shyly towards
Greg, in the same pew eight years, with the same
Yellow brown tie. They exchange smiles. "This church
Took me in and cared. Nobody else cared.
No one. Then Jesus took away my sin.
It rolled away….and now I am, now I
Am——"Free," our pastor whispers into his
Mike, in tears himself, as are many. The
Hurt of only knowing slightly, when you

Should know deeply, stings. A few seconds pass,
Very still. On a nod, Jason pinches
His nose and tilts his head, the pastor taking
Him in his arms, and after he has said
"In the name of the father, the son, and
The holy ghost," briefly dips him in the
Water. Once Jason is back on his feet,
Winds whip up high. "Praise Jesus! Thank you God!"
He bounds out of the tank and we can hear
A soul leap free forever. A child sees

This and sees the hand of the Lord wiping
Away all tears. Later, when age gives what

Brian Wood

You hope is wisdom, you think you're either
Lucky, born into a family who
Cares, or you have Jason's mother, in which
Case no sleep is ever sound enough. They
Don't baptize much in church now; people have
Moved on. Perhaps corruptible was always
A better fit. Or they have lost the eyes
Of a child, who saw grace falling all day
Everywhere, as snow deep in winter.

August 2015-March 2016

PIERCE BROTHERS WESTWOOD VILLAGE MEMORIAL PARK

You have to know it's there and no sign says
To remember or genuflect. The whole
Place is nearly cheerful—for a graveyard,
Since that's what it is, despite the laid-back
LA touches; most cemeteries fear
Or revere death; at this one, it's more like
An upscale career move. The cool kids are
At the back: Jack and Billy and Merv. They
Even do one-liners. "I'm a writer
But then nobody's perfect." The famous

And non-famous mix strangely. You walk by
An all smiles Don Knotts, whose large stone has small
Pictograms of his major roles, like he
Thought death would be a talk show; step over
An unmarked Zappa or Orbison, and
Stroll thru specific sections—Gardens of
Tranquility, Devotion, and, near the
Roses, Tenderness. To your left you find
Peace, Love, Remembrance; and in that order.
You wonder about prices; I find out

Brian Wood

Later that Devotion sells for one-third
More per square foot than Tenderness. If there
Is one place on earth that says "LA," it's
Here. The temptation to laugh at Knotts or
The pornographer from *Hogan's Heroes*
Is hard to resist, but I notice soon
That this ground isn't just an industry
Totem pole—real heroes are near. "Cut down
By rifle fire, Omaha." "Just after
Dawn, Killed in Action, Utah." "In manus

Tuas, Domine." The fake chapel seems
Odd on these lawns. And there is much else to
Lament here. Capote, wasting his gifts.
Monroe, gone away. Natalie Wood, just
Too sad, still, 30 years later. Peter
Falk, always funny and perfect for each
Role, and yet here he is anyway. No
Escaping this fact, even if millions
Know you, love you, wish you were still in films.
No escape if there is no one outside

Weekend Getaway at Generic Hotel

Your family who prays by your stone. No
Escape if you are unmarked or your grave
Is shared, near the trees delighting what they
Called Treblinka...Wilder was right to be
So cavalier. He had escaped death once—
Hitler's dogs were coming—and knew the run
Would end some day. Skip the pieties. Skip
The Polish town you came from; let someone
Else write the dates. Each light line of yours keeps
The dominion at bay, and the lilies
By your monument white as noon.

March 2014

Brian Wood

ESTABLISHED 32 AD, GIVE OR TAKE A YEAR

You wonder, wandering. This is the address
Of cool. UCLA has been Proudly
Smoke Free Since 2010, never mind the
Weed you see and smell, never mind the cars
Streaming past you, each one newer, sleeker,
Than the last. This place stands for free, learning,
Inclusive, shopping. This campus does not
Remind me of mine, slapped up next to a
Cold canal, where I studied in broad dull
Buildings, each one citing "God is the Lord

Of knowledge." Strolling on Gayley, I don't
See libraries, busts of Aquinas like
We had, lecture halls or labs, just mile and
Mile of chic shops and food and frankly, it
Could be for the best. At my old school you
Could still find Marxists, keep-the-faith profs who
Hated the U.S. so much they looked past
Kolyma, the show trials, the friendly
Confines of the NKVD. I admit…
I like this place more than I want to. No

Weekend Getaway at Generic Hotel

One here believes in a little red book
Or the killers who wrote them. The motto
Of this school is from Genesis but I
Bet the students don't care, and wouldn't know
The source. Doesn't matter: 'Let there be light'
Has no bearing if no one cares it's dark.
Even the (of course) fair trade coffee shops
Are silent as a cloister, everyone
Typing a screenplay. No books are open
And no one talks shop. Luther's circle is

Squared in Westwood. Each man his own priest—to
A flock of one. Each man interprets, for
Himself, the sacred texts he doesn't know.
His purity is whole: he only knows
What his phone tells him, and perhaps you could
Say the reformation is now complete
At Gayley and Weyburn, and I wonder
If it stings his shade, slicing deep, that he
Is as obscure here as Leo the tenth.

And yet for some certain books will linger.
You hear them in the tongues of those who read,

Brian Wood

And all the books they write show a mirror
To those same flames, shooting. The light from that
Fire could light the world. On my way home, I
Walk past Jews for Jesus, and here you see,
Finally, a book. The room is nicely
Full and they are reading, the sign says, Psalms.
Tonight is war again in Palestine,
And this evening I am all questions. I

Want to know—are they all Jews in there, do
They believe? Do they pray for home? Do they
Wish Israel was slower to anger,
Eyes fastened on peace? Are they as moved as
I am by their beautiful, strange book? "My
Help cometh from the LORD." Did Jews across
Germany or Poland recite these words
To themselves, coughing, death pouncing, as a
Smiling technician turned the gas way up?

Once you fall out of love the first time, part
Of you must hold back. I wonder if these
Jews for Jesus, established 32
A.D. or so, are hoping He can bring
What YHVH could not –peace over this earth.

Weekend Getaway at Generic Hotel

I suspect these people are torn: they know
That from too much blood may come Shoah; and
Have come tonight from fear, unable to
Flee past or future. You'd see so clear, and
Still be lost, not having seen the salvation.

July-August 2014

Brian Wood

THE PRESIDENT SINGS

You turn on the TV, hoping just this
Once there's something good on: you picked the wrong
Time: all of the stations have turned to a
Live feed of the President's speech, in South
Carolina, on this otherwise dull
Friday. He has come to mourn the dead. He
Has come to reason and he has come to
Speak plain. "A flag did not kill these good
People. Hate killed them; but the flag stands in
Part for our original sin. Our sin

Of slavery. It is time to atone:
Let us put up our swords: hate must not win:
Let us walk in the light of the Lord." By now
His country's leader for six years, he has
Spoken at too many mass funerals,
Folks killed because they were black, liked movies,
Or went to school that day. This man of words
Has clearly run out of them. There are long,
Long pauses between strophes. He is tired
Of saying what he said when the children
Were killed, that enough was past enough, and

Weekend Getaway at Generic Hotel

The murders must end. His eyes tell you he
Knows the race is over, that someone else
Will have to take the guns away from those
With death in their heart. He pauses... and then
Pauses again...a soul rent. Finally,
He ends an eloquent sentence by saying
Men are saved by grace alone. "Amazing
Grace." He repeats the phrase, head low. A few
Seconds pass, and his thin voice, a cappella,

Begins the famous hymn. He is not a
Singer and though the words are all as laid
Down, the music is not. Sometimes he is
Off pitch by quite a bit, so the church choir
And organist trill out a few notes to
Help him out. By the time he reaches "but
Now I see," the people as one body
Rise, clapping, singing, shouting. *Even so,*
Come, Lord Jesus. Emmanuel. God with
Us. We shall meet on that beautiful shore.

And you can tell the President would like
To join them, he'd be only too happy
To share in the victory, except he

Brian Wood

Has visited too many graven stones,
Had to make too many solemn elegies:
If the dead of Sandy Hook cannot change
His land, row on row of four foot coffins,
What will? He may now know that the prayers
Of his nation, yet though they come by tears,
And yet though they be fervent, availeth
Nothing.

July 2015

WHO ARE CALLED BY MY NAME

Right by the guy who swallows swords for cash,
Near the woman who takes a fee and sees
Your future with a deck of cards, over
By the medicinal reefer people,
Thirty feet from every kind of t-shirt,
With every kind of face and slogan, sits
"A Shul By The Beach." My wife, thinking I
Don't see, grins when I kind of wander in,
Knowing I won't quite enter. A small sign
Says that I'm at the Pacific Jewish

Center, Ocean Front Walk, Venice. I am
Cordially invited, by notice and
Voice, to see new paintings for sale by the
Synagogue. Another sign says they teach
Hebrew in five weeks. I chuckle at this,
To myself. (Learning the language takes years.)
Three people, taking pity on my strange
Posture, invite me in and smile when I
Nod, knowing I mean "No, thanks." "The art is
Quite good," they say by way of mild comment,
And again I nod, meaning "No." I can't

Brian Wood

Explain—to my wife or them—why I am
Standing there, reading pamphlets. I could ask,
I guess, if their faith was any help at
Chelmno, if he who laid the foundations
Of the earth cared a whit. Instead I glance
At the little history they provide,
Saying the shul was once just part of a
Thriving Jewish culture, but that a move
To the suburbs, "and air conditioning,"

Took their toll. But they're doing better, and
Next year, say by Shavuot, they plan to re-
Do the kitchen. My father, brought up miles
Away from this creed and Venice Beach, can
Share their lament. "As a child my parents'
Church was full on Sunday nights and often
You could not get a seat. God poured out
His spirit…It would be so warm by nine. But
TV came along… and Ed Sullivan,
And…" He trails off, not wanting to finish.

If we said kaddish for our dead, would they
Recognize our half-baked clichés, our loose
Compromises? My father's people breathed

Weekend Getaway at Generic Hotel

The air of Pentecost and chose instead
An evening with plate spinners and foot jugglers.
In the synagogue they spoke with a flame
Who led them from Egypt, and instead they
Chose someplace out in the burbs with high def
And AC. Are they still peculiar,
Called by His name, if the shul is just one

More groovy vendor on the beach? And those
Who once sat in wonder, their eyes fixed on
Cloven tongues like as of fire, can now pour
You a mean latte, at a better price
Than Starbucks. And if we no longer cared
For worlds passing, or what is to come, we
Might ask how wisdom came to mean what we
Say, and knowledge what we do, and it all
Became easy somehow, with the answers
Right here, waiting, on the tips of our tongue.

June 2014

Brian Wood

WEEKEND GETAWAY AT GENERIC HOTEL

You know the kind: you've stayed there too. One bar
Of scratchy soap, and two scratchy towels
Tucked out of sight. If you'd like ice, grab your
Map and go get it. Your room does include,
Gratis, a view of some…deals being made
In the parking lot: you'd call the front desk
To complain, but they seemed unhappy when
You checked in, like you spoiled "No Guests Weekend."

When we wake, I ask Rachel what she dreamed
About. "I was married to a better
Man and we were in a better hotel.
I'm going for a walk." I do the same,
And when I amble past the just-plain-folks
Coffee shop, I see signs for New Hope Church;
They meet in conference room B every
Sunday at ten. Beneath the name I can

Just make out 'Turn Your Eyes Upon Jesus.'
At that, mind leaves body, and it's thirty
Years ago, and I am helping my dad
Set up his Sunday school class, at R.B.

Weekend Getaway at Generic Hotel

Barn across the street from our church. Adult
Bible Study 1(a) had grown too large,
So he taught in this dive instead. He'd bring
My brother too, and we'd help clear tables

And make space for a small lectern. Funny
What your brain captures, what it lets go. He
Must have then sent us to our own classes,
While he read Paul again, and his students
Heard 'But some are fallen asleep' in a
Room full of stale beer and old smoke gone flat.
That night, dreaming, I am at our old church,
And singing, as we often did, Turn Your

Eyes Upon Jesus. When we finish, the
Woman who wrote the hymn sits beside me,
And strangely the child I was speaks. 'This tune
Is so pretty but seems sad, and calls out
Longing.' Small lights flash off her cool eyes. 'The
Wonder that I feel is easy—can I—'
You can ask. What I know you may not like.
'I was scared. I did not want to hear that

Brian Wood

The world was dying.' The eyes soften. *My*
Song was not for children. Maybe your
Parents should have let you stay home. 'What did
You mean, there was no light in your darkness?
Is that life in sin?' *Adults can write true*
Words that to a child ring false. Each day was
New to you, as it should be. For me, the
Things of this world were thin. I lived sparely.

Unless I looked full in His wonderful
Face, I fell. My sight failed and my husband
Left. What little I had would get smaller
Still. I'd tell people 'I am fine in the
Things that count,' yet only think of falling
Asleep. My heart wrote the tune and that's why
It cuts, a soul in lamentation pealing.

When I wake up, Rachel gleefully tells
Me my snoring woke three adjoining rooms.
She laughs for a good long time and says she
Will treat for breakfast, just not here. "I love
You too," I say, pretending to be cross.
She laughs again and this time we both do.
On our way to check out, she says—"Who goes

Weekend Getaway at Generic Hotel

To church at this dump?" "I'm....not sure, really."

I could tell her what she might guess. Some are
Here because they have to or feel they should.
A few more are hoping to see the high
Bright fires of Pentecost, some want to not
Be at home, and still others are here since
The little things they asked of life, like a
Love abiding and rivers of living
Water, stayed somehow just out of reach.

August-October 2014

www.ingramcontent.com/pod-product-compliance
Lightning Source LLC
Chambersburg PA
CBHW060532030426

42337CB00021B/4226